A Woman's Guide to Bikes and Biking

A Woman's Guide to Bikes and Biking

Julie Harrell

A Cycling Resources book,
published by Van der Plas Publications,
San Francisco

Copyright © 1999 Julie Ann Harrell
Printed in U.S.A.

Published by:
 Van der Plas Publications
 1282 7th Ave.
 San Francisco, CA 94122
 U.S.A.

U.S. book trade sales:
 Dan Haldeman & Associates
 Watsonville, CA

Cover design:
 Kent Lytle, Alameda, CA

Photography:
 Cover photograph by Bob Allen
 Photograph on page 37 by Katherine Mittnight
 Photographs on pages 38, 74, 82 by Cheryl Ruhman
 Photograph on page 39 by Bill Reitzel
 Photograph on page 72 by the author
 All other photographs by Neil and Rob van der Plas

Publisher's Cataloging in Publication Data
Harrell, Julie A.
 A Woman's Guide to Bikes and Biking.
 p. cm.
 Includes bibliographical references and index.
 1 Bicycles and bicycling—handbooks and manuals.
 I. Authorship.
 II. Title.
 L.C. Card No. 98-61191
 ISBN 1-892495-11-2 (paperback original)

Acknowledgments

Mahalo to Tony Tom, Gravy, Barry London, Dave Miller, Rob van der Plas, Gary Fisher, Steve Potts, and Joe Breeze. You showed me the sweet trails, waited for me at the top of the mountain, and taught me what I know. Mahalo to A Bicycle Odyssey; The Spoke; Clifton Park Sports; Mud, Sweat, and Gears; and Wilderness Trails Bikes for access to your shops, bicycles, and time. Finally, I'd like to thank Belle Marko for her patient modeling, and Elaine at *Dirt Rag* magazine for regularly publishing my work.

Disclaimer

The author does not accept any liability for decisions made by you, and recommends you work with your local bike shop to assure proper fit and acquire other safety information. A helmet should be worn while cycling, but cannot eliminate all risks. You are responsible for your own safety.

About the Author

Julie Harrell has worked in the bicycle trade since 1982, when she began road racing as a very poor undergraduate in Oklahoma and Texas. She regularly raced the Hotter 'N Hell One Hundred, finishing the third annual race in 5 hours and 20 minutes. After winning the Oklahoma Grand Prix in 1986 on the same $200 road bike, she decided to continue working in the trade in order to afford the best bikes and tools.

Julie has a Master of Science in Technical Communication from Rensselaer Polytechnic Institute, and is now a freelance writer, editor, and webmaster. She writes articles and stories, both nonfiction and fiction, for publishers in the fields of bicycling, metaphysics, and health. She also works as a bike shop consultant, helping local shops improve their business practices. She spends time each summer in the San Francisco Bay Area, riding bikes with old friends, hanging out in coffee shops, and catching up on the latest industry news. She still likes all-day rides with lots of climbing, and enjoys an alternative, vegetarian lifestyle.

She lives with her husband Mark, daughter Reesa, three dogs, and two goats on eighteen acres in upstate New York. She builds and repairs all the family bikes, as well as those of her friends, and hopes to someday own a titanium Wilderness Trails Phoenix mountain bike. If you have any questions, comments, or stories you'd like to share, her E-mail address is: gabriella@taconic.net.

Foreword by Belle Marko

When I decided to reenter the world of mountain biking in 1994, I figured it would be easier to find the right bike than it had been when I built my single-speed klunker back in 1976. In the olden days, if you wanted a cool bike, you had to put it together yourself. But with all the great new bike technology I'd heard about and seen, I thought I could just go buy a bike off the showroom floor and take off.

Was I in for a surprise. There was plenty of technology, but that made my job harder, not easier. In the olden days, I had to make a few decisions; now there seemed to be hundreds of decisions to make, and I was overwhelmed. Not only did I have to choose a brand, but the burley shop guy wanted to know what kind of material I wanted: chromemoly, carbon fiber, aluminum, or titanium? How about the components: LX, XT, XTR, or XYZ? It was all gibberish to me. He wanted to know what size frame I wanted, what kind of riding I'd be doing, and how much money I wanted to spend.

Dazed, I walked out of the shop, too intimidated to tell the shop guy that I had no idea what he was talking about. Off I went, scratching my head.

But I didn't give up. I really wanted to ride again. A month or so later, after talking to lots of friends and test-riding lots of bikes, I finally settled on a production bike that felt right.

Little did I know that this was only the beginning of an ordeal that finally led me to the bike I ended up with. By the time I was totally satisfied with my bike, I had changed the stem, the seatpost, the handlebars, the pedals, the grips, the bar-ends, and the tires.

Then came the whole part about what to wear, what to eat, what tools to carry, and how to use them. After a long process, and many mistakes, I am finally loving my bikes. Yes, I have two: a road bike and a mountain bike. And I went through the painful and expensive process with both.

When Julie told me she was writing this book, it thrilled me to know that it would mean women looking to buy a bike wouldn't have to go through what I did. If I had had this book when I started this venture, it would have saved me a lot of time, money, and frustration. I could have been riding comfortably on a bike that was right for me all along.

I hope this book will shine a light on the mysterious world of bikes and biking and give you the confidence to walk into a bike shop without feeling like a dork, and walk out with the right bike and accessories that fit you and your riding style. You go, Girl!

Contents

Introduction

Cycling is for women. You can become a proficient cyclist, regardless of your weight, age, fitness level, and previous experience. These factors all come into play, of course, but if you can ride a bike, you can become proficient at cycling. This book was written to help you find the best bike and other equipment for your needs, and to help you become (more) proficient at using it.

First and foremost, you must venture out and find a bike shop that will help you fulfill your dream of becoming a confident, experienced cyclist. The right bike shop will take time to answer all of your questions, fit you properly to a bike within your price range, and offer you several models to test-ride before you make your final decision.

This book is a tool to help you. With it, you can decide what type of bicycling you want to do. Learn what to look for in a quality, woman-friendly bike shop. Size yourself properly on a bike that will fulfill your needs. Purchase a bike within your price range and ability level. Find the proper accessories, equipment and clothing. Learn how to accelerate, shift and brake properly. Safely ride your bike in a variety of settings. Have your bike serviced at the bike shop.

Within these pages you will discover the shopping secrets that enable so many women to purchase and ride the bike of their dreams. True, a quality bike shop will give you information over time, and I encourage you to ask questions, but if you want to learn the details all at once, this book is your ticket to ride. After you read this book, you will walk into the shop fully informed and prepared. You'll be able to browse by yourself if the salespeople are busy with other customers. This happens occasionally. Personal service sometimes involves a brief wait for your turn.

I do not recommend you shop anywhere besides a bike shop. Mailorder and big box stores do not provide the personal touch. In an age where large, impersonal organizations are taking over from small businesses, privately owned bike shops still exist as local employers who put capital back into their neighborhoods. They often sponsor racing teams, allow young people to work part-time after school, and add quality to a community that may otherwise be dominated by the big box chain stores. You sometimes pay a little more for your bike, but the rewards are great.

You may ask yourself, "Why should I spend from $230 to $3,000 for a bike when I can go to the local big box or discount store and get one for only $100?" Is supporting my local independent retailer worth spending $130 extra? Well, my answer to that is, you get what you pay for. If a bike shop could sell a $100 bicycle that consistently worked properly, didn't fall apart at the slightest stress and bump, and didn't require constant maintenance for parts that never worked properly in the first place, they would gladly do so. The bottom line is, it cannot be done. There are no good bikes out there in that price range, period. I've been in the business for 15 years, and can honestly tell you not to shop for a bike anywhere that doesn't specialize in bikes. You'll end up throwing the $100 piece of junk in your garage, and never touching it. Or, you'll attempt to have it repaired at the local bike shop, and end up spending up to $90 just for a tune-up. We see it all the time.

Go ahead and buy all of your equipment at a bike shop, preferably the same one where you buy the bike. The bike industry as a whole is not a high-profit industry, and most, if not all, bike shop owners are in the business because they love the sport and the people who are attracted to cycling.

Support your local shops, and they will still be around for your children.

Read this book and get the real lowdown on buying a new bike. You will learn how to talk to bike salespeople and mechanics about whether or not you need a full-suspension bike, one with front suspension, or a hardtail, a hybrid or a road bike, and what to do with the bike once you buy it. Remember, the bike industry may seem to still be male-oriented, but we women are a group who can benefit the most from cycling. We take care of the family, shop for the groceries, help our children grow into responsible young adults. Cycling is a great way to do something nice for ourselves, lose weight, participate with our children on family outings, and lower stress in our lives.

1

What's New About Bikes?

New women bike buyers today are often overwhelmed at what seems to be the choice of too many complicated bicycles, when all they want to do is pedal to the gym. "Who needs 21 gears, anyway?" "Why can't a person just get a one-speed that will go uphill?" "I just don't need 21 gears. It's much more than I need." "I just don't have time to learn all this." We in the bike business hear this every day, and these objections are all valid.

I will try to simplify the mystery of today's bicycle, its gears, and its parts. First of all, shifting gears today is not difficult to learn. Secondly, you need gears to go uphill. If you can program your answering machine, you can learn to use the gears on your new bicycle.

Bike Types

The bikes we'll discuss here are all multi-speed machines. They use derailleur systems, which means that the gears are shifted by means of little mechanisms (derailleurs) that move the chain sideways between differently sized cogs and chainrings. You select a low gear to go slowly uphill, a high gear to go fast downhill, or an intermediate one for any type of terrain in between.

These bikes also have hand-operated brakes. They have hand levers instead of the old type that was applied by pedaling backward to stop.

They all have front and rear derailleurs, right and left shifters, front and rear brakes, and left and right brake levers. Fig. 1-1 on page 17 shows these parts, which you'll find in one variant or another on all the bikes discussed here.

When you buy a bicycle with a 21-speed derailleur system, you are also purchasing specific types of systems. Here are the types you will find on bikes in bike shops.

Shifters

For bikes with flat handlebars, such as mountain bikes, the shifters may be the Rapid-Fire variety, located under the handlebars, or of the Grip-Shift type, consisting of a handgrip with a rotating mechanism. On drop-handlebar bikes (mainly road bikes), you'll find either STI shifters, integrated with the brake levers, or conventional shifters installed on either side of the frame's downtube. To use STI-type shifters, push the lever towards the side and it shifts, pull it towards you, and it brakes.

Brakes

On flat-handlebar bikes, you'll find either V-brakes or cantilevers brakes. V-brakes are a simple, yet effective design. Cantilever brakes are the older style. Adjusted properly, either type will stop your bike even in adverse conditions.

Derailleurs Gearing

Although all of the bicycles I advise you to test ride have derailleur gearing, some of them may vary in type. The derailleurs are very similar, but the brakes and shifters may be different.

One item that is becoming increasingly popular is the use of a triple crankset, formerly found only on mountain bikes, but now increasingly finding its way onto road bikes as well. The crankset is the mechanism in the middle of the bike with the chainrings and the cranks, on the ends of which the pedals are installed. If there are two chainrings, it's a double crankset; if there are three, it's a triple.

Bikes with a triple crankset (three chainrings) and, say, eight cogs on the rear wheel's cassette are referred to as 24-speed bikes because theoretically you could use each of the 3 times 8, equals 24 resulting combinations.

Fig. 1-1 The controls: gear and brake parts, also showing the crankset.

Right gear shifter

Right brake lever

Rear brake

Front derailleur

Rear derailleur

Left gear shifter

Left brake lever

Front brake

Crankset

In reality, you will not choose to engage each and every one of those theoretically possible combinations. Think of it this way: If your car has a standard transmission, you don't necessarily need to use your first, second, and third gear, except to get going. The bicycle is similar. If you start off in an easy gear, you will immediately shift to a harder gear once you get going. The greatest difference between the car and the bicycle is that the car will increase your waist, tummy, and rear measurements, while the bicycle will enable you to lose padding.

Frame Materials

When buying a bike, even as an integral package, you are buying the frame first. It's the most expensive element of the bike, sort of a skeleton for the interchangeable parts. The frames of stock bikes are generally made of chrome-moly, aluminum, titanium, or carbon fiber.

Steel

Steel frames, in order of pricing, are either plain high-tensile steel, part high-tensile steel with a chrome-moly seat tube, part high-tensile steel with a chrome-moly front triangle, or full chrome-moly. The cheapest one, the one with the full high-tensile steel frame, sells for around $200 and is slightly heavier and less responsive than the part chrome-moly (a stiffer, lighter blend of steel) frame. At this price range, the difference is very slight.

The bike with a full chrome-moly front triangle will perform noticeably better off-road than the high-tensile steel bike, and slightly better on road. The reason is, a chrome-moly front triangle allows you to fully apply each pedal stroke, rather than have it dampened by heavy steel. This bike is usually in the $350 to $400 price range without front suspension. A full chrome-moly frame will be lighter and less fatigue-inducing than a heavier steel frame because it is quicker to respond to pedaling, steering, and braking. Bikes with full chrome-moly frames are in the $450 to $650 price range.

Tubing diameters varies from one manufacturer to the next. Lighter frames often have slightly oversized tubing, but not always. Some lighter chrome-moly frames have more bottom bracket flex than others, which means when you pedal uphill hard, your crank moves slightly inward and touches the front chainring. Heavier women should ride bikes with less bottom bracket flex, while lighter women can ride a flexy bike because it won't affect their pedal stroke very much.

Most chrome-moly frames are TIG-welded, and some come with beautiful lugs and not so beautiful gussets to reinforce the stress points where one tube meets the next. You'll notice when you look closely at the frame that there seem to be extra welds near each corner of the frame. That's a gusset. Gussets are generally found on aluminum frames, but sometimes appear on chrome-moly frames as well.

Aluminum

Aluminum frames are often built with oversized tubing to compensate for the material's inherently low rigidity. Some aluminum frames were once bonded, but the manufacturers discovered that TIG-welding worked just fine and did not require the extra sleeves that are needed for strong bonds. Aluminum frames are oversized, and depending on the bike, they may be extremely oversized. Really fat, thin-walled tubing will give you a super stiff ride, which is great for climbing but hard on the bones when descending. Aluminum frames are generally constructed out of 6000- or 7000-series aluminum. They come on bikes that cost around $400 for a low-end model without front suspension. If you can afford it, I suggest buying at least a $600 bike, because once you get into that price range, the frame will be of good quality and the components will work fairly well too.

Carbon Fiber

Carbon fiber bikes combine the best of both worlds. They are stiff enough for effective climbing, have no bottom bracket flex, and don't beat you to a pulp on the downhill. On top of all that, they are lighter than most steel and aluminum frames. Pricier too. Carbon fiber bikes usually run you at least $1,000. They are considered "high-end," as opposed to "low-end," recreational bikes and mountain bikes.

Titanium

Titanium frames are quite expensive, but worth the cash if you can find one that doesn't flex. There are great welders today still putting frames together by hand, one at a time. On these frames you can expect to find fine craftsmanship, fillet brazed joints, and seamless welds. If you can afford it, or later on in life, if you fall totally in love with cycling, treat yourself to one of these beautiful and indestructible frames. Expect to pay up to $3,500 for a sweet frame and fork. You'll have it for a lifetime.

Components

High-end and low-end also describe the Shimano component gruppos that appear on the majority of stock bikes today. Gruppos are the component groups, comprising parts such as derailleurs, hubs, shifters, pedals, and brakes. Stock bikes are those you buy right off the store room floor, much as you would buy clothing from a department store. Specifying a particular frame with particular parts, piece by piece, is called "spec-ing" your bike. This word is pronounced "specking," and you will hear it often around the shop. You may even want to "spec" your own bike, complete with a hand-built frame designed with your physical dimensions down to the last centimeter. That's usually done with road bikes.

Components work together and allow you to shift, brake, accelerate, and steer. A low-end bike will have low-end components, much as a less expensive car will have a less expensive steering wheel, engine, wheel set, and everything else. Low-end components aren't a bad thing—they just don't perform nearly as well as high-end components. For example, when you shift gears on a $300 bike, you'll notice a definite difference between that experience than when you shift gears on a $600 bike.

More expensive models operate in a smoother, quieter manner, and if you are riding off-road in technical situations, you sometimes need to shift fast, or "dab." Dabbing means touching your foot to the ground to break your fall. Why break when you can shift? Quick shifting allows you to make sudden decisions, such as whether to jump that log or walk over it. Quick shifting allows you to ride uphill rather than walk. I recommend higher-end component gruppos for technical Singletrack, because you never know what you'll run into on the trail, and you had better be ready for surprises.

Suspension

A common facet of bike shop conversations is mechanical discussion. Guys like to talk about what amount of travel their full-suspension bike has versus the front suspension hardtail, or how much damping the oil shock has versus the spring coil and air shock. All this stuff may be important to understand for them, but you'll probably never service your shock yourself, so you don't have to deal with it. As long as you buy a good one that feels great when you ride it, don't worry too much about whether you have 3 or 4 inches of travel when you descend.

We will discuss sizing in Chapter 4, which will enable you to drop by the local shop and size yourself properly on whichever bike you want to test ride. Your main concern here is, if you decide to buy your bike at this shop, whether or not it's funky, how are they going to treat you?

2

Which Bike Fits Your Style?

There are several distinct main categories of derailleur bicycles on the market today: mountain bike, hybrid, road bike. Mountain bikes are available in several different types: recreational, with or without front suspension; aggressive hardtail, with or without front suspension; full-suspension, cross-country or downhill. Although there are also slight differences between various road bikes and hybrids, they can all be described adequately within their main categories.

Each type is engineered with a very specific purpose in mind; some overlap, some do not. I will describe the various styles, how much each costs, what it does, and what type of rider would want to purchase it. You may discover that my explanations differ slightly from what you may have read in advertisements or claims made by popular bicycling magazines. Keep in mind that you are about to get a bird's-eye view from a very opinionated woman who rides all types of bicycles. I hope it helps you make your final decision. At least you'll be more informed.

Mountain Bikes

Mountain bikes are the most prevalent machines on the market, and there are a number of different sub-categories: recreational bikes, cross-country bikes, and downhill bikes.

Recreational Mountain Bikes

The recreation bicycle usually costs from $230 to $500. There are several subgroups of recreational bicycles, all of which have a wheel diameter of 26 inches. First, I will describe what similarities all of these bicycles share, then I will describe their differences. All styles have 21 or 24 possible gear combinations, of which you will actually use five to eight when shifting properly. They are equipped with triple cranksets, which facilitate wide-range gearing, and either cantilever brakes or V-brakes.

Recreational bikes have an upright handlebar position, with a rise in the handlebars themselves. More expensive models will have a complete crome-moly frame, rather than a partial chrome-moly frame (heavier and less responsive). The component gruppo will be mostly Shimano, with either

Fig. 2-1
Recreational
mountain bike.

GripShift or Rapid Fire index shifting, cantilever brakes, or V-brakes on more expensive models (quicker response from two-finger brake levers), and a comfortable seat. All come equipped with semi-slick mountain bike tires, which work well on the road, and not very well off-road, but adequately for flat dirt paths.

Recreational bicycles sometimes come equipped with a flex-stem that absorbs shock from the road, and now you can even buy one with a seatpost shock absorber. Very comfy.

If you want to sit upright and ride a very stable bicycle on pavement, bike paths, or non-technical dirt and country roads, you will choose the recreational bicycle with the upright stem and handlebars, rather than the bike with knobby tires and a flat stem. This bike will not climb well under any circumstances, because of the rider's upright position. It will not descend well on steep downhills either. The relaxed frame and parts are designed primarily for comfort, rather than performance. This doesn't mean the bicycle isn't a quality machine. It is great for cruising flat roads, easy hills, and mellow neighborhoods.

The difference between recreational bikes and regular mountain bikes in the $230 to $500 price range is that a regular mountain bike may or may not have an upright stem with flat or upright handlebars. They rarely have a comfortable seat, but do perform better off-road than the above-mentioned recreational bikes. Often, the regular mountain bike has knobby tires, and the rider's torso will be more extended over the top tube, which allows for quicker handling in technical situations. You will find yourself in a less upright position, leaning farther over the top tube to hold onto the handlebars.

Aggressive Hardtail Mountain Bikes

The mountain bike without suspension in the $400 to $700 price range can be considered an aggressive hardtail. Hardtail simply means without suspension. These bikes place the rider in a more stretched-out position, which allows her to climb and descend in a controlled manner. These bikes are not built for absolute comfort. They are designed for technical trail riding.

Mountain Bikes with Front Suspension

Many mountain bikes come outfitted with front suspension. Whether you are buying a strictly recreational bike or an aggressive off-road bike, you may find that you like the idea of a kinder, gentler ride due to shock absorption. Suspension forks are the most commonly found type of front suspension. If you buy a bike with suspension forks, the telescoping forks have the ability to dampen any rough spots of your ride by using spring elements and some form of damping. Sometimes, they use a combination of two to three different methods to achieve optimal performance. As bike prices go up, the amount of damping and travel your fork will allow increases, which means if you hit a really big bump, like a street curb, your fork won't bottom out.

Headshocks are only found on one make of bicycle (Cannondale), as they are patented by that company. Unlike suspension forks, they cannot later be added to a bicycle that was originally equipped with a rigid fork. The headshock differs greatly from front suspension forks in performance, appearance, and overall feel of the bike. Many people who have started out mountain biking on rigid forks, and many roadies (people who love road bikes) prefer headshocks over suspension forks. The reason is that the entire spring assembly is hidden within the head tube, while the fork itself remains rigid.

As a result, the bike handles like a hardtail (mountain bike with no suspension), without the heavier front end and larger fork. You will also discover that the rigid frame design of the bike with a headshock, combined with one-directional damping (only the steerer tube, inside the head tube, moves, as opposed to the situation whereby the two sides of the front fork move independently of each other) results in a much firmer ride, with just enough shock absorbing ability to make your ride easy and sweet.

Another facet of the headshock is your ability to increase or decrease the amount of damping you require while riding the bike. If you are a larger woman who rides gnarlier trails with bigger rocks, larger ruts, or taller logs, you may want to change your headshock's damping capacity to better negotiate these obstacles. The damping dial is located on top of the headtube (where the stem meets the bike frame), and is quite handy if you are hammering uphill with a bunch of guys and need to turn the knob quickly. The reason you may do this is, when climbing uphill, you rarely need to use the headshock at all, so it's nice to decrease or completely eliminate the suspension capacity of your bike, rather than

Fig. 2-2 Front suspension mountain bike.

bounce uphill with each pedal stroke. You will think you are riding a hardtail, and pass those who cannot control the damping on their suspension forks without stopping first.

Suspension forks appear on $400 bikes, but the forks themselves can cost up to $600. Headtube shocks begin on bicycles that cost $500, depending on the model and gruppo that comes with the bike.

If you only have $400 to spend on a bike, I recommend bypassing the suspension, and going for a hardtail. It is always wiser to buy a better frame and components than a low-end gadget on a low-end frame. A $600 bike with front suspension will give you a full chrome-moly or aluminum frame, along with a decent fork with enough travel and not too much flex when you brake and corner. Headshocks begin on aluminum bikes that cost around $600.

Adding Suspension

You may want to buy a bike with a rigid frame and fork now, and add a suspension fork later. That is fine as long as you realize that adding a new fork is expensive, because the price of individual forks is higher than the price difference between a new bike with and without a suspension fork. Unless you are an experienced mechanic with the correct tools, or you have extra money and you really don't know if you want front suspension right away, buy the bike with the fork already installed. You'll get a better deal, won't have to wait long for your bike while the shop orders the correct parts, and will already have a bike designed to work with a particular suspension fork.

The headshock cannot be installed on any other bike than that for which it was originally designed, so if you want a bike with the headshock, you must purchase the complete set the first time around.

If you are physically in shape, and do not suffer any type of back, arm, or wrist injury, you can comfortably cruise around town without any type of suspension on your bike. People have been riding rigid bicycles of the current general design since 1885. However, if you do experience bodily pain when you hit a bump on the road, or if you want to scream down Singletrack trails at an inadvisable warp speed, front suspension will decrease your likelihood of early exhaustion due to rough road conditions. It will increase your ability to negotiate technical trails at a faster speed. I suggest you first learn how to ride trails slowly, without suspension, before you go too fast down drop-offs and hurt yourself. Even though suspension was originally developed to improve handling and speed in highly technical situations, it has evolved into a method of achieving comfort without sacrificing safety.

Full-Suspension Bikes—Downhill and Cross-Country

Full-suspension bicycles usually begin at the $850 price range, and go up from there. Front suspension or rigid fork bikes are called hardtails, which means the rear triangle of the bike

Fig. 2-3 Full-suspension mountain bike.

(and the seat tube area where you sit) is stiff. Full-suspension bikes engage several methods to move the rear triangle, offering the rider a truly comfortable ride, similar to that of a scaled-down motorcycle with no engine and narrow tires. Your seat is suspended in a variety of ways, as is the rear wheel. This provides a bike which can speed downhill at beyond warp speed, negotiate unusually technical areas with little skill on the rider's part, and otherwise increase one's comfort while riding at a normal speed.

Cross-country full-suspension bikes are light and suitable for climbing as well as going downhill fast. They are best used on technical trails that require more than front suspension only.

Downhill full-suspension mountain bikes are designed for riders who do not plan to pedal uphill. They have more travel, meaning the ability to absorb larger bumps at a higher speed, than cross-country full-suspension bikes. They are generally heavier than cross-country bikes and best used on ski slopes and other assisted rides.

Full suspension became popular with the majority of riders when downhill mountain bike racing began to get television coverage. Some racers reach speeds of over 60 miles per hour, which I certainly don't recommend for even the most advanced riders, because if you crash, well, full suspension won't dampen your impact. On the other hand, if you like to ride at ski resorts, many of which now offer lift services for bikers in the summertime, you can enjoy a truly fun experience on your full-suspension bike. There are models that offer up to 5 inches of travel on the front and rear, which means your bike can bounce a controlled 5 inches per bump. Because of the unique damping design of full-suspension bikes, the bounce will be like riding in a car with good shocks, rather than a car with worn-out shocks. These bikes are especially designed with downhill racing in mind, but can be enjoyed on the local mountain at a leisurely speed.

Another seldom discussed but valid advantage of a full-suspension bike is for people who have arm, back and neck injuries, or older people who aren't as limber as they used to be. They can ride these bikes comfortably. A rigid bike requires you, the rider, to absorb each and every bump, in your arms, wrists, legs and back (if you are sitting). Good riders can flex their legs and bend their knees to accommodate the rough ride, but an older person, or someone with a debilitating injury, will discover that full suspension allows them to ride farther and longer with less pain and more enjoyment. You really do not need full suspension if you are only going to ride on the road.

Hybrids

Hybrids combine the frame design of a recreational mountain bike with slightly thinner tubing. They have narrower wheels than mountain bikes, with the same diameter as road bikes (700 mm), flat or upturned handlebars, an upright stem, cantilever or V brakes, and triple crankset with mountain bike gearing. Advertisements once claimed that the hybrid could go both on the road and off-road, but the hybrid

Fig. 2-4 Hybrid.

actually is suitable only for riding on smooth trails and roads. Since high-end hybrids come equipped with front suspension, you can get comfortable on your bike. Even the least amount of road fatigue is filtered out, and you enjoy a smooth ride.

Road Bikes

Road bikes are a breed apart. They were the mainstay of European racing and cycling for many years. They are used only for the road, and usually have a double crankset, rather than triple, although many manufacturers are recognizing the advantage of triple chainring gearing. High-end road bikes have a light, racy frame, and can be ridden long distances without tiring the fit rider. Road bike wheels are 700 mm, but rather than having a tire width of up to 38 mm, as with hybrids, they generally come equipped with tires that are only 19 to 25 mm wide. Road bikes have drop handlebars, which place the rider in a stretched-out position over her bike. This facilitates climbing and riding into head winds, and allows a much more aerodynamic position all the way around.

The gear shifters on road bikes are located either on the downtube or on the handlebars (integrated with the brake levers, and referred to as STI by Shimano, ErgoPower by Campagnolo). The advantage of STI and ErgoPower shifting is, you do not need to take your hands off the handlebars to shift up or down, and since the road bike is a very technical machine, requiring maximum steering at all times, this is a very real benefit. Downtube shifting, on the other hand, has been around for years and will probably be around for decades longer. Experienced riders have little difficulty reaching down with one hand to quickly shift into another gear.

Road bikes generally begin at around $400 and go up from there. If you can afford it, I highly recommend you spend at least $1,000 for your road bike. This is a machine that requires a serious investment to achieve maximum performance, and although there are many quality road bikes out there, once you reach the $1,000 price range, you are looking at a really nice ride.

Road bike frames are either steel, aluminum, carbon fiber, or titanium. Some steel frames, although not all, have a narrower diameter tubing than the tubes used on aluminum frames, and "give" when you are riding, which means you enjoy a ride in which the bike will absorb some of the bumps. Custom steel frames, on the other hand, are generally stiffer than the stock steel frames, and do not give much at all over road bumps, which means your body must absorb what your bike does not. When climbing uphill, you will experience less bottom bracket flex on a heavier steel frame than on a lighter steel frame. Steel has the ability to give and/or provide a stiff ride if the tubing is a certain diameter and thickness.

Many aluminum bikes, although not all, have fatter diameter tubing with thinner walls, which increases bottom bracket stiffness. In simple terms, when you pedal hard uphill, your crank won't flex. When you hammer fast downhill, you'll get slightly beaten by the stiff bike. Aluminum bikes with large-diameter tubing do not give when you hit bumps, but narrower diameter, heavier-walled tubing is a bit more comfortable. You sacrifice comfort for performance, however, and road bikes are all about performance.

Titanium frames are rare, and are often hand-built to spec, which means your frame is built for your body. Some, not all, are less flexible than others. Find a titanium welder who knows how to build a bike that is stiff, fast, light, and built to last. Plan to pay over $2,500 for the frame alone.

Road bike frame designs usually have a steep seat tube and shorter chainstays than most mountain bikes, which places the rider in a stretched-out position over the top tube. Another road bike frame design has a more relaxed seat tube angle. This position places the rider over the seat and rear of the bike, facilitating a comfortable ride and easy handling. The aerodynamic position of all road bikes facilitates climbing, descending, accelerating, braking and steering. When you go shopping for a road bike, be sure to find a bike shop that specializes in these light machines so you will be fitted properly.

Other Types of Bikes

There are a number of categories of derailleur bikes that you won't find in every bike shop but are worth mentioning here. These include the touring bike, the recumbent, and the hand cycle.

Touring Bikes

Touring bikes generally have dropped handlebars, along with a multitude of braze-ons for racks and other accessories. The

Fig. 2-5 Road bike.

touring bike will take you long distances over paved roads. Frame geometry is relaxed, increasing your comfort. Touring bikes are not so relaxed that they don't climb well—they just climb slower than road bikes. You can put fat, 38 mm tires on your 700 mm rims, which is usually the wheel size specified for touring bikes. Three chainrings and low gearing allows you to pull a heavy load up mountains, while the stability of a good touring bike keeps you on a straight line during descents. If you want to ride 50 miles or more with lots of stuff, this may be the bike for you.

Recumbents

Recumbents are two-wheeled bicycles that allow the rider to sit in an alternative position rather than on top of the saddle with arms outstretched. These bicycles have a dedicated group of aficionados, but most people have never seen one in a bike shop. The advantages of recumbents are their lower aerodynamic positioning, which allows the rider to reach higher speed more easily. This is also their disadvantage, because they are not as visible as traditional bicycles, and must rely on a tall flag flapping in the wind, which somewhat hinders the aerodynamic positioning and offers more wind resistance. Recumbents are priced from $1,500 to $4,000 or more, and can be found in pro shops on the East and West Coast, and wherever there is great interest in alternative cycling machines, such as around university campuses.

Hand Cycles

Hand cycles are the machines of choice for differently abled people. The rider sits comfortably near the ground, using her hands to pedal opposing cranks. Gearing is the same as on regular bicycles. Steering is achieved by leaning either to the right or to the left. Hand cycles are priced from $1,900 to $4,000 and up, and can be ordered by any bike shop that takes an interest in serving the large population of differently abled people. I highly recommend them for women who do not have full use of their legs, but would like to get out there and spin with the rest of us.

3

Finding the Right Bike Shop

A good bike shops shouldn't be hard to find. You may have one right down the street, and think that you don't because the guys play heavy metal music, the clothing rack has dust on it, or the greasy, loud-mouthed mechanic in the back sports a nose ring and you absolutely can't stand nose rings. A good bike shop may seem like testosterone territory

Fig. 3-1 Julie with the staff of Clifton Park Sports in Clifton Park, NY.

where only macho guys with shaved legs and neon jerseys hang around, swapping crash stories and admiring their scars, and a woman can never enter.

Types of Shops

A good bike shop may be that little hole-in-the-wall that doesn't sell tricycles, has European road frames hanging in the window, and a bathroom that smells like, well, someplace to be avoided. A good bike shop can also appear as a sparkling, well-lit place with beautifully polished wood floors, artfully marketed displays, clean bathrooms, and a staff with matching polo shirts. You aren't looking for appearances here, although they certainly help. You are looking for people who know what they are talking about, and are willing to share that information with you. You are also looking for one year's service warranty on a new bike, which includes the basic tune-ups for one year after purchase.

The typical bike shop with a management that rides with the employers, supports its local race team, and employs people who dress in an alternative manner, may not fit into the conservative model one expects to find these days in

Fig. 3-2 Paul and Dave help Julie find the right bike at The Spoke in Williamstown, MA.

contemporary shopping. A brightly lit, finely tuned shop with all the sparkles of a large, corporate department store may seem more inviting to the first-time bicycle buyer. You don't have to look far to find a good bike shop. You just have to look carefully.

Great shops treat their customers with respect, take the time to answer questions, and enjoy repeat business from loyal customers. They also employ people who love to ride, which does cut into shop hours, making them slightly less accessible to people who can only shop on Sundays. Truly great shops may look like grimy bike messenger hideaways on the outside, but if you look carefully, you will discover a wealth of information right beneath your eyes. So go ahead and stroll into the shop that strikes your fancy, whether it is a clean, well-lit place, or a tiny roadie hangout. You are now about to become armed with the conversational tools you require to negotiate your way into the bike of your dreams.

Let's talk about terminology. Do you want to ride on the road, off-road, technical Singletrack, or cruise the neighborhood bike paths? Should you first take a peek at recreational bikes, mountain bikes, hybrids or road bikes? Are

Fig. 3-3 Tony Tom, owner and road bike expert at A Bicycle Odyssey in Sausalito, CA.

you interested in hardtails, front suspension, rear suspension, or a really stiff road bike?

Shop Knowledge

First impressions, as I said earlier, can be deceiving. The very woman-friendly owner may be out buying cappuccinos and donuts for the surly mechanic who greets you at the door, or doesn't greet you at all, which is sometimes the case. Go ahead and stick around, check out the bikes, and see what they seem to be selling. Is it mainly mountain bikes, or mainly road bikes? Do you see any obviously used bikes that don't seem to be having repairs, but are parked around like little pet cats? Those probably belong to the staff. Are they mountain bikes or road bikes?

Your initial inspection will tell you more about the shop if you toss any preconceived notions of how the shop should appear. You are more interested in whether they really know much about bikes, whether they all ride or not, and what they ride. If you are in the market for a road bike, you should find a shop that specializes in road bikes. There should be several parked nearby that look as though they are for sale or currently in use.

Since you will be fully prepared to size yourself on a mountain or road bike, you won't be relying entirely on the shop to size you correctly. However, road bikes are so specific that you truly need a highly qualified person to measure your shoulder width, arm length, torso length, and standover height. Otherwise you will end up with a road bike that almost fits. Unless someone in the shop actually rides a road bike, don't plan to purchase one there. The shop may be a perfectly nice, reputable place, but roadies are a breed apart, and it usually takes one to size one.

4

Proper Fit On Your Bicycle

Women used to have great difficulty finding a bike that fit right off the store room floor, because most mountain bikes, and many road bikes, were designed for men. In general, women have longer legs, a shorter torso, and shorter arms than men of the same size. Mountain bikes were once designed with long top tubes and long stems, which meant that the average woman would be stretched-out beyond her comfort level on every mountain bike she tested.

These days, manufacturers realize the buying potential of women, and have taken care to create bicycles with a shorter, sometimes downward sloped top tube, shorter stem, and shorter seat tube. Even so, you need to know a few rules before you assume every bike shop employee will automatically fit you perfectly to your new bike. We'll begin with the easiest bike to fit, the mountain bike. My advice to you is, before you enter the first bike shop, purchase a tape measure with inches and centimeters. You'll need it to measure bikes for yourself, and to assist the sales people, should they need it, in measuring your standover height, leg length, arm length, and shoulder width.

Fitting the Bike

Mountain bikes, road bikes, and hybrids usually come in sizes specified by inches. These sizes represent the distance between the top of the seat tube to the center of the crank, the top of the top tube (measured at the seat tube) to the center of the crank, or the center of the seat tube to the center of the crank. Sounds complicated, but it's really not. The seat tube length will be directly proportional to how much standover height you have. If you can straddle the bike, leaving at least 2 inches of crotch clearance between yourself and the top tube, the bike basically fits. Not all bikes fit equally, though, so you need to know a little more about your own size.

Road bikes are sized using centimeters for more exact measurements. The rules are similar: look for 1½ inch standover clearance, sit with a 90-degree angle between your upper body and your arms when grasping the hoods of the brake levers, and most of all, get comfortable on your bike.

Standover Height

Standover height is easily measured by taking a contractor's square (metal L-shaped measuring device) and standing

Fig. 4-1
Measuring the bike's top tube length.

against a perfectly plumb, vertical wall. You hold one leg of the L between your legs, until it touches that most sensitive part, with the vertical leg of the L lying vertically down against the wall. Have someone measure from the top of the horizontal leg of the L to the floor, and you will have your exact standover height. This measurement will make your search relatively simple. Rather than depend on the sometimes confusing measurements offered by various bike manufacturers, you can simply take your tape measure out and check for yourself. You'll need at least 1½ inches standover height clearance for your road bike, and 4 inches for your mountain bike.

Different Sizing Methods

Some bikes fit better than others. Manufacturers often size their bikes differently from each other, further confusing the prospective bike buyer. You will discover that an 18-inch bike may really have a 17-inch seat tube, measuring from top of

Fig. 4-2 Measuring Belle's standover height.

the top tube to the center of the crank. The extended inch or so of seat tube found on some, not all, mountain bikes, will have no bearing whatsoever on the actual fit of your new bike.

Thus, if you are approximately 5 foot 7 tall, you will most likely ride a 17.5-inch or an 18-inch bike. The 17.5-inch bike may be measured from the top of the seat tube, making it really a 17-inch or a 16.5-inch bike. This bike will fit fine if you don't have extra long legs, like I do. If you have extra long legs, with a 34-inch inseam, you may need to buy the 18-inch bike, which is really a 17-inch or a 17.5-inch, depending on where it is measured.

If the other manufacturer measures a 17-inch model from the top of the seat tube, adding an extra inch, you may think since you ride an 18-inch in one, you ride a 17-inch in another. Close enough, right? Well, not exactly. The 17-inch model will actually be closer to a 16-inch if it has been measured from the top of the seat tube. This bike is too small for you.

Fig. 4-3 and Fig. 4-3a Measuring the bike's seat tube top to center.

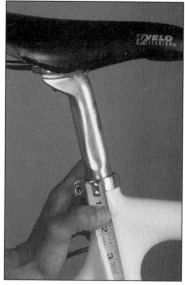

How can you tell if a bike is too small or too large? First, know your standover height. Then, straddle the bike that seems closest to your physique. If you have a couple of inches to spare, you can at least presume the bike isn't too large. However, if you feel incredibly crunched up when you test ride it, unless the stem is really short, you may need to test ride a bike by another manufacturer. Bicycles are rarely unavailable in all sizes, but the shop itself may be low on a certain size because they had a busy weekend, or you may be one of those in-between people who are going to almost, but not quite, fit two different sizes.

An example of this sizing problem is a woman who is 5 foot 8 with a 30-inch inseam, or a woman who is 5 foot 6 with a 32-inch inseam. Both women will fit either a 17-inch or an 18-inch mountain bike if they have an average torso length for their height. Since a 16-inch mountain bike is usually more like a 15-inch, I don't recommend that size for anyone over 5 foot 5, unless she has an inseam of 29-inches or less.

The 5 foot 8 woman will not have much crotch clearance on an 18-inch mountain bike, and feel crunched up on the 17-

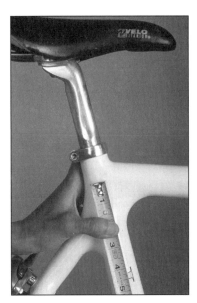

Fig. 4-4 Measure the bike's seat tube from center to center.

inch bike, which will allow for plenty of clearance but not enough top tube length to accommodate her long torso. The 5 foot 6 woman will comfortably straddle the 17-inch bike, but need quite a bit of seatpost showing to accommodate her extra long legs.

Each woman needs something special to make that in-between bike fit. The 5 foot 8 woman will require a longer stem on the 17-inch bike, should she choose to ride it, or a shorter seatpost on the 18-inch bike. The seatpost that is spec'd with the 18-inch bike may not insert deeply enough into the seat tube to accommodate her need to lower the seat. The 5 foot 6 woman will require a longer seatpost on the 17-inch bike to stretch her long legs, or a shorter stem on the 18-inch bike to accommodate her shorter torso.

Fig. 4-5 Dropping a plumb line from the top of the shin bone to the pedal spindle.

Rules to Remember

You need at least 2 inches of crotch clearance from the top
tube to comfortably ride your mountain bike off-road. Road
bikes require less crotch clearance. These bikes need to be
fitted even more carefully because you will be locked into one
position for longer periods of time. The mountain bike allows
you to use various hand positions, which are different from
those used with dropped handlebars.

Stem and Brakes

Your stem should have a slight rise, with enough horizontal
length to allow you to feel comfortable. You should not feel
too crunched up or stretched-out when grasping the
handlebars. Your handlebars, on a road bike, should be
between 2 and 4 inches wider than your shoulder width. On a
mountain bike, you may find initially that wider handlebars
make the bike easier to handle. Eventually, narrower
handlebars that accommodate your shoulder width will be
the most comfortable. When you grasp the brake levers on
your mountain bike, they should fit nicely into your hands

Fig. 4-6 Belle
seated at the
ideal 90-degree
angle, with
correct leg
extension.

without undue stretching on your part. If they do not, have the shop adjust the brake levers on the handlebars, or reduce the distance of the brake levers if you have small hands or short fingers.

Saddle

Your saddle should be exactly level. While riding, you should not be seated toward the rear of the saddle, nor on the tip. I advise a comfortable (not huge, fat, or otherwise overly cushioned) saddle that is designed especially for fit women riders. Search until you find the right one for you. They are simple to remove from the seatpost, and if the saddle doesn't work right, nothing else will either.

4-7 Julie measures Belle's arm length.

4-8 Julie and Belle: same height, different measurements.

Seatpost Position

When first adjusting your seatpost length, find a position that will allow you to sit with your leg almost fully extended, with a slight bend in the knee, while riding. To find this adjustment, first place your foot on the pedal, with the ball of your foot exactly flat, while the pedal is horizontal. Place a plumb line at the bony protrusion located at the bottom of your knee cap and the top of your shin bone. When dropped, it should directly intersect with the center of the pedal spindle. Adjust the saddle either forward or backward to achieve this line. If your seatpost is too extended, your hips will rock from side to side when you pedal. If your seatpost is not extended enough, your knees will have more bend, which can cause muscle strain and other problems.

Ideal Position

The ideal position places your body at a 90-degree angle when measured with arms locked. Some people like to sit more upright, while others want to be more stretched-out. The 90-degree angle is optimal. This means that while you are seated and riding the bike, your arms are at 45 degrees, and your legs are at 45 degrees.

If you prefer to initially ride in a more upright position, remember that you sacrifice climbing efficiency and offer greater wind resistance, which will lead to earlier fatigue. You can always change your stem as your riding ability improves, thus achieving the preferred 90-degree angle at a later date.

Pedals

When you have comfortably fitted your new bike to your body, the next decision to be made is whether or not to buy clipless pedals. These pedals do not come with the traditional toeclips. Instead, your shoes clip into the pedals. Should you decide to go clipless, as many people do these days, you must learn the proper pedaling technique to avoid damaging your knees.

A few hints: Find pedals that allow for "float," which enables your foot to move around horizontally upon the pedal. Try to keep your feet as close together as possible. This means you need to find a crank set, pedals, and shoes that do not place your feet too far apart. If you are used to wearing high heels, you can either relearn how to place your foot horizontally on the pedal, or have the bike adjusted to accommodate your different stride.

5

Choosing Accessories

In order to have a fun ride, you have to first be comfortable on your new bicycle. Some accessories are basic, mandatory items, others are optional. As you log more miles on your new bike, you will discover that accessories enable you to stay out on the bike longer, with less discomfort, and greater independence. Begin with the essentials, then gradually add to your inventory until eventually you have everything in this chapter.

Accessories for the Rider

First we'll look at the things you get to wear yourself, while in the next section you'll learn about the things to install on the bike.

Helmets

Wear a helmet. They come in all colors, shapes and sizes, and require proper fitting, which you can do yourself. Choose the first helmet off the shelf that fits into your color preference, price range, and style. Expect to pay from $30 to $150. Most shops will give you a discount if you buy your helmet when you buy your bike.

Try on the small, medium, and large to see which one fits the best. Then, place the helmet directly over your head, with at least some of your forehead covered. The helmet should fit between your eyebrows and your hairline. Next, place the straps closely around your ears, with the clasp meeting under your chin. Ask someone to gently tap you on your helmeted head. The helmet should remain in place. If it does, it fits.

Hats

A tight-fitting hat or cap under your helmet will keep you warm and absorb sweat. In the summertime, you can use a simple bandana. Either item will work well, keep your helmet from slipping, and really mess up your hair. Oh well. Fashion can't always win.

Fig. 5-1 Choose your favorite helmet.

Shoes

Proper riding shoes are necessary, whether or not you ride very often. If you do not use clipless pedals, you can ride in any comfortable walking or hiking shoe that has a stiff sole. Cycling shoes cost between $50 and $250, which, as you can tell, is a large price range. A sturdy shoe with few frills will cost around $80. Plan to purchase a pair if you do not own something comparable. Riding in tennis or other soft-soled shoes is not good for your feet, and will severely limit your riding ability.

Cycling shoes will save your feet from becoming sore and even injured from too much pressure on the arch and ball of your foot. If you ride clipless pedals, you must choose a shoe that accommodates the cleat for your particular pedal. Ask the bike shop which pedals and shoes go together. Most people who ride mountain bikes prefer mountain bike shoes. They have a rugged sole and allow you to traipse through the woods with your bike. Road bike shoes, on the other hand, are not meant for walking. They are designed to be the lightest, most elegant part of your cycling apparel, and will increase your pedaling efficiency. Unfortunately, if you do

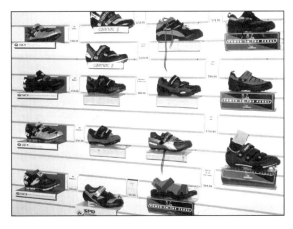

Fig. 5-2 Shoes, shoes, and shoes.

attempt to actually walk while wearing road bike shoes, you will waddle like a duck.

Shorts

Cycling shorts come in all different shapes and sizes, although the traditional black short is still quite popular. Expect to pay between $30 to $100 for a decent pair of shorts. If you have ever ridden several miles in a pair of jeans, you understand why a large seam in the area where your crotch touches the saddle is an impossible discomfort. Tight cycling shorts allow maximum leg movement with little or no added wind resistance. The inner chamois which protects your crotch is designed so that you can wear the shorts without underwear. Even though you may feel as though you have a huge diaper between your legs at first, the chamois quickly becomes your best friend on rides more than a few miles long. Always wash your shorts after every ride. Chamois creme is available should the shorts liner become stiff or otherwise uncomfortable.

Tights

Tights fit over cycling shorts, and allow you to keep your knees warm on chilly morning or evening rides. Tights cost $15 to $100 or more. You can find leggings at department stores for light, cotton tights, while the heavier versions should be purchased in a bike shop. The cotton pair will do fine for the spring and fall, while heavy wool or other thermal material will allow you to ride on cold, wintry days. Many tights have extra material at the front to protect you from buffeting head winds during particularly cold times.

Jerseys

A cycling jersey is another accessory that adds immeasurable comfort to your ride. These garments are designed with fabric that fits skin-tight, wicks moisture away from your body, and keeps you cool in the summer, warm in the winter. Jerseys are priced from $30 to $150. Most have nice pockets on the back where you can stuff your extra jacket, food, wallet or other items you want to keep handy. Jerseys are longer in the back than the front, to cover the rider's back over her shorts. They also fit tightly in order to decrease wind resistance. If you've ever experienced the noisy flapping of a loose jacket while riding your bike, you'll truly appreciate a well-cut jersey.

Fig. 5-3 Julie checking out jerseys in an aisle full of jerseys, shorts, and tights at a bike shop in Sausalito, CA.

Fig. 5.6 Great cycling gloves with lots of padding to protect the nerve endings in the palms of the hands.

Other layers to add include a wind-resistant outer shell, and another layer of a wicking fabric, fleece or wool. This combo will keep you comfy for the long rides.

Gloves

Cycling gloves are designed and especially padded to protect the ulnar and median nerves in the palms of your hands. They also protect your hands should you suddenly experience a nasty spill. Cost is usually between $20 and $60 or more, depending on what style you buy. Winter gloves are more expensive than summer gloves. Look for lots of padding in the palm.

A good cycling glove has a terry cloth outer piece which allows you to wipe your nose. Until you learn the one nostril nose blow, fashionably carried out by experienced cyclists, you must rely on your gloves to keep your nose clean. Long-fingered, short-fingered, and no-fingered gloves all work fine, as long as they grip well, have padding, and of course, absorb moisture.

Snacks

Bike shops usually sell some type of energy bar or gooey substance designed to digest quickly and give you energy. These cost between $1 and $2, depending on whether you buy the gooey or the chewy versions. Try a few different flavors until you find one that suits you. The benefit of these energy enhancers is that you will rarely experience an upset stomach if you eat them while riding. They fit nicely into your jersey pocket or bike bag, don't usually contain lots of fat, and are pre-wrapped. The disadvantage of quick energy items is that some taste like cardboard, while others taste like toothpaste. Try before you buy.

Bike Accessories

Your bicycle will run just fine if you carry nothing at all, but you really need to have water, a snack, and perhaps your keys and wallet. Some women carry cell phones too, which I think is a great idea. To haul all of your stuff, find a small seat bag and attach it under your seat. This can carry your basic items. Bags cost between $15 to $50, not including the really big ones, which I think are more cumbersome than helpful.

Water Carriers

Water bottle cages attach on the downtube or seat tube, and will carry your water. They cost around $7 to $10 for a simple cage. Water bottles are $2 to $5, so this combo is quite affordable.

I have had success with a hydration system that you carry on your back. This narrow bike backpack holds a 70-ounce water bladder with a protruding hose that fits neatly in the front strap. The pack itself holds an extra jacket, food, wallet, keys, and a spare inner tube. If you take long rides, this is the way to travel. No water bottle cages or bouncing water bottles. Easy access, which eliminates reaching for the water bottle on the downtube. Copious amounts of liquids in the hottest days of summer. Your thirst will be permanently quenched. You pay more for these systems, which cost from $50 to $100. They are well worth the expense if you ride long distances, ride off-road, or drink lots of water.

Bar-Ends

Bar-ends are those horn-like protrusions that fit onto mountain bike handlebars. They allow you to change hand positions, and increase your climbing ability when standing up out of the saddle. I highly recommend them, whether you are a beginner or an experienced rider. Many people assume the bar-ends should tilt upward to accommodate an upright riding position, but this is not the optimal way to use your bar-ends. Have them installed pointing forward and tilted up at only a 10- to 15-degree angle, so you will bend over more while holding them. This will allow you to either become more aerodynamic when speeding downhill, or give you greater pulling power when climbing uphill. When adjusted at the correct angle, bar-ends allow a more comfortable ride, and protect your hands from fatigue. They only cost between $20 and $40, and are well worth the price.

Racks

Rear racks usually install on the seatstays, although now you can also find racks that install on the seatpost. Front racks are used for touring, and can only be installed if you have a touring bike with the proper braze-ons that allow rack installation on the front fork. Here I will primarily discuss rear racks and their various uses.

A sturdy rear rack will cost around $40 to $60. You may use either a bungee cord for basic carrying, a bag especially made for the rack, or panniers on your rear rack. People who commute to work or ride in areas with changing weather often find the rear rack indispensable. Rather than carry a bunch of stuff on your back, you can let your bike do the carrying, and further enjoy the ride. The only objection to rear racks is purely aesthetic. They just don't look as cool as a bike minus the rack. Full-suspension bikes may have difficulty accepting a rear or front rack, and I would not advise putting one on your fancy road bike either. Rear racks are a utility item, very useful, and often ignored in favor of heavy fanny packs or backpacks.

Lights

Lights are absolutely essential if you ride in the early morning, during twilight hours, or at night. Expect to pay from $30 to $250 for a good front light. Rear flashers are around $15 to $20, and work quite nicely at making your bicycle more visible.

Front lights come in less expensive disposable battery types, or more expensive rechargeable battery types. The less expensive lights don't put out anything near the light of the rechargeable models. If you do any night riding at all, I highly recommend investing in a rechargeable set of lights. You will be able to see little switchback trails, and if you are on a road bike, cars will see you very well. One type of rechargeable battery light puts out 32 watts of power, which lights up everything around you. These last for years and years, don't pollute, and help keep you safe in the dark hours.

Locks

If you ever leave your bike anywhere for even five minutes, plan to lock it up tightly, and expect to watch it carefully. U-locks, cable locks, chain locks, or just plain locks work better than no lock, especially in cities where bikes are hot items. Expect to pay from $20 to $75 for either the basic lock or a heavy motorcycle-type lock. Most people use U-locks, but ever since I discovered how easy it is to break a U-lock, I have resorted to the thick cable lock with protected housing and a clasp that cannot be easily broken. If you find yourself stranded and just have to go inside a building, casually walk your bike in with you. Use your helmet clasped around a wheel to foil any quick escapes by would-be thieves. Flip your bike upside down and release both wheel skewers too. That way, at least you'll have a chance to catch anyone who tries to just ride off into the sunset with your favorite steed.

Fenders

Fenders are handy if you ride in an environment where there is even a small amount of water present. Your rear rack often serves nicely as a fender, depending upon the manufacturer (some rear racks do not have a solid middle, rendering them useless as fenders). Front fenders either clip or bolt on, while rear fenders attach to the seatstays or the seatpost. Front and rear fenders may cost from $20 to $40 apiece. Unless you want a muddy line up your back, or nasty road grit in your teeth, fenders are the easiest way to stay clean and dry while pedaling through wet muck.

Cyclometers

Cyclometers function as speedometers, odometers, and clocks. They can measure your trip distance, total time elapsed, average miles per hour, top speed reached during the trip, and revolutions per minute (RPM) while pedaling. These handy gadgets are priced from $25 to $90, depending on the number of functions of each model, and the brand. I recommend buying one just to measure your cadence. The optimal spinning cadence rhythm is 90 RPM. This is primarily advised for those who have a high fitness level and want to achieve optimal pedaling efficiency. Spinning increases your fitness level, raises your cardiovascular workout, increases your heart rate, and doesn't damage your knees. You must use a cyclometer with cadence capacity to measure your pedaling speed in RPM.

Heart-Rate Monitors

Heart-rate monitors are a combination of a band around your chest, in close proximity to your heart, and a little computer on your bike or wrist which measures your heart rate at all times. These cost from $100 to $150, and can be found in pro bike shops. The heart-rate monitor is useful, once again, if you are a high fitness level athlete, and want to ride at your maximum heart rate without going over or under it. Another use for the heart-rate monitor is for people who may have experienced illness in the past, or those with heart problems. Most heart-rate monitors will beep or emit some type of noise when the maximum heart rate has been achieved. Since you set the maximum, it can be high or low to accommodate your physical fitness level.

Trailers

Bike trailers are the only safe way to transport your child. There are many makes and models available, some for as little as $175, others for as much as $450. Whether you are heading out for a few hours in the neighborhood, or a few days on the highway, the bike trailer will keep your little one tightly cinched into a sturdy vehicle that will not roll over if you somehow wreck your bike.

Bike trailers have many advantages over all other ways of transporting children. Even the heaviest, least expensive models are incredibly safe compared to other options, such as child carrier seats which attach to the front or rear of the bike. If your child is one year old, you are ready for a bike trailer.

Look for a trailer with a roll-over bar that surrounds the plastic or aluminum frame. The roll-over bar operates as a protective shell which will not collapse on the child, should you somehow flip the trailer completely over (very unlikely). Your trailer should have two straps which go over the child's shoulders, one across his/her waist, and one between the legs. This type of system will hold your child in place even in the most dire circumstances, should you lose control of your bike.

Most, if not all, bike trailers have a rotating hitch that will turn if you turn your bike. This hitch allow you to, once again, lay your bike down on the road, while not affecting the trailer's upright position at all. Compared to all other means of transporting young children, the trailer is the finest, safest, and easiest to use.

Once your helmeted child is strapped in tightly, you can easily pull the trailer, maneuver corners, and ride up- or down-hill. Trailers are also handy for stashing supplies, such as extra diapers, clothing, food and water. As you can tell, I wholeheartedly recommend trailers for hauling children. After your child has reached age four or five, you can still use the trailer for touring, rather than depending upon cumbersome panniers. Another advantage of many bike trailers is that they will double as strollers, with the addition of a conversion kit.

Tools

Whether or not you know how to repair your bicycle, if you have the correct tools, you may get lucky and run into someone who can. Of course, I recommend learning how to repair everything yourself. Beginning your ride with the proper tools is the first step to total independence. You'll need the following:

- ❑ Pump or CO_2-inflator
- ❑ Allen wrenches from 2 mm to 7 mm
- ❑ Spoke wrench to fit your spokes
- ❑ Chain tool
- ❑ Extra inner tube
- ❑ Tire lever

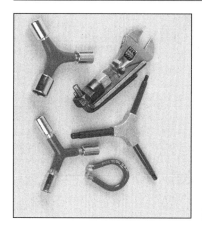

Fig. 5-5 Tools to take along.

❑ Small screwdriver

❑ Small adjustable wrench

❑ Small hand pump

With these tools, you can fix most of the common problems that usually occur while riding. Chains break, tubes go flat, cables stretch or become lose, derailleurs get out of adjustment, brake pads fall off. Even if you can't fix it yourself, having the right tools will enable you to either figure it out, or get some assistance so you can ride your bike home.

6

How to Ride Your New Bike

Now that you've purchased your new bike, had it fully accessorised, and are suited up and are ready to ride, let's take a moment to review the parts on your machine. You have the basic bike frame, the wheels and skewers, the seat and seatpost, the brakes and levers, the derailleurs and shifters. This package of fun will take you many miles to see many sights, as long as you remain safe and it continues to work properly. Before starting up for a day's ride, it may be a good idea to go over a few basics.

Safety Check

Take a look at your wheel skewers' quick-release (QR) levers. Are they tight? You don't want your wheels to fall off on some great downhill pass, so double check the quick-release levers. The QR lever should be flush with your bicycle's fork and rear dropouts. Twist the thumbnut on the other end of the skewer while holding the lever until you can still fold the lever toward the hub. Fold it inward toward the bicycle. It should fit snugly against the fork and dropouts.

Stand in front of the bike, holding onto the front wheel with your legs. Try to twist the handlebars one way and then the other. Do they stay put, or is your stem bolt loose? Tighten the bolt with an Allen wrench if it is loose. The handlebars, like the skewers, should fit snugly in their headset.

Bounce the front wheel on the pavement. Do you sense or feel a rattle or vibration in the front end of the bike? If so, your headset may be loose. Adjusting a headset can be tricky, but with the right tools and a good repair book, you can do it youself.

If your bike's front end rattled, and it wasn't the headset, your wheel hub may be loose. Adjusting hubs is an exacting science that requires proper tools and a little bit of knowledge. You can do it if you want, or take it to the bike shop.

Fig. 6-1. The names of your bicycle's parts. Although shown here on a mountain bike, the same names are used for parts of a road bike.

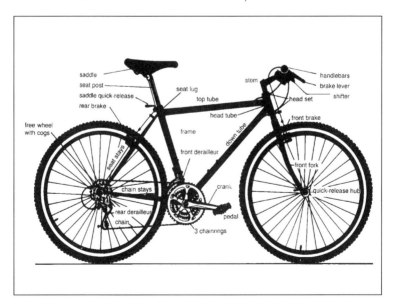

Spin the wheels while observing their rotation through the brakes. Do you see a wobble, or is the wheel actually hitting a brake pad? Time to get that wheel trued, another exacting science requiring the proper tools and knowledge. While you are checking the wheels for wobble, pull the brake levers and see if the brake pads really hit the wheel rims, or if they actually hit the tire. You know what to do if they are off. Get out your tools. Call the shop.

Check the crankset/bottom bracket area for play. Grasp both crank arms, and pull them from side to side. Do you detect any play or vibration of any kind in the bottom bracket area? Does the crank creak when you pedal? Time to adjust those things before you ride. Get out the book, the tools, or the phone.

You are almost ready to ride. After a brief journey into the world of the derailleur, we will head out into the sunshine, helmeted, with tires pumped up. First the gears. Why are they here, and what do they do?

Shifting Gears

The single most confusing aspect of both mountain bikes and road bikes is the gearing system. Many women who are not familiar with the cycling world find themselves put off at the thought of riding a 21- or 24-speed bike. I'd like to dispel a myth here and now. The bike with 21- or 24-speeds doesn't really allow you to use all of those gears. At least half of the possible combinations are not advisable, and you'll probably only use about five to eight combinations. The large range of possible gear combinations is only there so the derailleurs can easily move the chain from one spot to another.

I'll start at the beginning so you will become more confident about your bike's gearing system. Take a look at the handlebars. Follow the cable that begins at the shifter on the left side of the handlebar. This cable will lead to the front derailleur, located on the seat tube of the bike. The front derailleur's job is to move the chain from one chainring to the next. That is its entire reason for existence. Anytime you move the left shifter from one spot to the next, you move the chain with it.

The front derailleur moves the chain over two or three chainrings, which are located on the right-hand crank. Two chainrings are commonly found on road bikes, while three chainrings are usually on mountain, hybrid, touring, or other recreational bikes. The reason why you need a front derailleur and two or three chainrings is simple: to ascend and descend at approximately the same cadence, or pedaling rate, measured in revolutions per minute.

Back to the handlebars. Follow the right shifter cable down to the back wheel, where it connects with the rear derailleur. This rear derailleur looks more complicated, and it is a bit larger than the front derailleur, but it does basically the same thing. It moves the chain from smaller cogs to larger cogs on the cassette, which is that set of small rings on the rear wheel. The chain must go over the derailleur pulleys at all times, which keeps the chain lined up properly with the front chainrings too. If you shift the right shifter in any direction, you will be moving the rear derailleur either up or down the cassette, from cog to cog.

Here's a little tip: Never combine the large chainring with the large cog in the rear, or the small chainring with the small cog in the rear. These combinations are inadvisable but physically possible. If you fear you have shifted into the wrong gear, just look down at your chain while astride your bike. If the chain is in a straight line from front to rear, you are in the clear. If the chain is diagonally crossed, you are not in the right gear.

Riding in the small chainring and the small rear cog can be disastrous, because there is not enough chain tension on the rear derailleur to keep it taut, which means your chain can slip at any time, forcing you down onto the pavement if you aren't careful. Riding in the large chainring and the large rear cog will place too much tension on your rear derailleur, eventually breaking it. This necessary component will have to be replaced at considerable expense.

Remember, small goes with large, and large goes with small in the world of front and rear derailleurs. The small chainring up front combined with the large cog on back is your climbing, or "granny" gear. The largest on the front and the smallest on the rear is your downhill, or "hammer" gear. The ones in between are for cruising mostly flat areas. You'll find your most comfortable gears, and use them regularly, once you are used to the whole concept of shifting.

When shifting before a sudden uphill, or attempting to shift down because you have already begun an ascent, try to first pedal one full revolution and propel yourself a few feet. While coasting uphill for that brief second, quickly shift down, pedaling very gently. The trick is to momentarily stop applying pedal pressure by briefly coasting uphill. Anyone can do it with practice. You'll avoid the crunching sound of someone abusing her gearing system by attempting to simultaneously pedal hard and shift.

Once you have the hang of shifting gears, your cycling experience will become easier and more fun on a daily basis.

Braking Techniques

Braking properly also requires a bit of practice, so I'll briefly go over the proper way to use your brakes. On a recreational bike, mountain bike, hybrid, road bike, front suspension or full-suspension bike, you always need to use the right-hand brake lever first, which corresponds to the rear brake. Apply gentle pressure to this brake before squeezing your left brake lever, which corresponds to the front brake. Never lock your brakes. Your tires will skid and you may lose control of the bike.

Since the brakes on all new bikes have improved
dramatically in the past five years, you can expect to plunge
over the handlebars if you apply the front brake first. Another
safe braking tip is to not use your brakes while cornering
unless you absolutely must. If so, use the right-hand lever
first, applying gentle pressure.

Accelerating

Accelerating is easy, once you get the hang of it. Place your
bike in a gear that is suitable for the terrain you are about to
ride upon. If it is flat, the middle chainring and the middle
cogs will work fine. If you are just beginning to ride, stay on
the flats for this exercise. Straddle your bike, place one foot on
one pedal, then pedal forward. Sit on the seat, add your other
foot after you have rolled a yard or two, then you will be
cruising. To dismount, roll almost to a stop, then move off
your seat onto the pedals, just as you did while accelerating.
Once stopped, put one foot on the ground first, then the
other. Never dismount from the seat directly to one side. Your
position on the seat is such that you will possibly fall if you
try to simply lean over.

A Useful Mountain Biking Technique

One method of riding over bumpy fire roads and other
obstacles is to stand up in the pedals, crouched over the
handlebars, with your seat grasped between your legs. As
you encounter each bump, allow your knees to bend, flexing
your legs so they can absorb the shock. If you are riding
downhill, first lower your seat slightly, then crouch behind
the seat if the terrain is extremely steep. As you roll downhill,
your weight will remain behind the handlebars, keeping you
from pitching forward in an "endo."

The Basics

Obey all the rules of the road. Avoid heavily congested roads. Tell people where you are going just in case you don't make it back. Look around you at all times. Don't tailgate cars or other vehicles of any kind, including bikes. Yield the right of way to pedestrians. Make eye contact with drivers before riding through intersections. Watch out for suddenly opening car doors. Do not wear a radio on your head. Beware of dogs. Always wear a helmet.

Have fun, treat your bike right, and it will treat you even better. When it becomes damaged or worn out, take it to the bike shop and let the mechanics do their thing.

7

Where to Ride Your Bike, and Why

Y ou now own a new bike, have a basic understanding of how it operates, and know what type of riding you want to do. Let's take a closer look at exactly where you can safely ride, how far, and for how long.

Recreational Bikes

If you choose the upright recreational bike with semi-slick tires described on page 24, you will do well to ride on bike paths, around the neighborhood, or in the city. The upright position is quite comfortable for short distances. This bike is for fitness and enjoyment, not necessarily high performance.

Since you are sitting upright, your position on the bike does not lend itself to much climbing, or at least, serious climbing. Nor will you go very fast in this position, because aerodynamically your body is like a sail in the wind. Riding around the neighborhood in a relaxed manner will keep you fit, enable you to flex your muscles, and not give you a back or neck ache. The lack of knobby tires on your recreational bike gives it less rolling resistance, making it easier to ride smoothly over pavement. The smaller diameter 26-inch wheels lend greater stability to the bike. For ten miles or less, the ride will be smooth and easy. After ten miles, you may feel fatigued until you are used to this style of bike.

One difficulty in riding recreational bikes is the lack of aerodynamic positioning. Even though the upright position feels comfortable at first, you will soon discover that your body operates as a huge sail, slowing you down during even the slightest head wind. As you become more proficient at riding your bike, you may wish to change your handlebar stem and add bar-ends to the handlebars. This minor part replacement will place you in a position closer to that of a roadie or mountain biker, allowing you to ride faster, longer, and harder without undue fatigue.

Hybrids

Hybrids are pretty much the same story, usually more upright than hard-core mountain or road bikes, but quite comfortable for city riding. The hybrid will go faster than the recreational bike, even though you are still riding upright.

Fig. 7-1 Reesa learns the finer points of cycling from her godmother, Cheryl.

Hybrids typically come equipped with 700 mm wheels, larger in diameter and narrower than the 26-inch wheels used on mountain bikes. They use flat mountain bike handlebars and the same type of brakes and gearing, so you will have a wide range of gears available. While faster on the flats, the hybrid does not climb much better than the recreational mountain bike. However, if you have no large moutains around, and you really want to speed down the paved roads, your hybrid can pick up a respectable speed. After about 25 miles you may get tired.

Hybrids combine road bike wheels with a relaxed mountain bike geometry. They operate optimally on paved roads only, as the relatively narrow wheels are not suitable for dirt or singletrack riding. You can ride your hybrid around town or on bike paths, using it primarily for fitness or as a commuter bike.

If you want a more stretched-out position on your hybrid, replace the stem with a model that has more reach and less rise, meaning it puts the handlebars farther forward and not as high up. This enables you to climb more efficiently and ride longer distances with less fatigue. Bar-ends are also a great accessory for your hybrid to make it more versatile. As on the mountain bike, they should be installed almost horizontally, angled up only about 10 to 15 degrees.

Hardtail Mountain Bikes

In the beginning, there were one-speed bikes, bouncing and rolling at warp speed down gnarly fire roads with laughing crazy people barely hanging on for their lives. Then there were road bike derailleurs, attached to heavy one-speed frames so the laughing crazy people could ride uphill too. Afterwards, the mountain bike took over, rocking America and Europe with its stylish sashay onto dirt and singletrack. Now the hardtail mounain bike is almost a forgotten breed, though it's built to last forever with a minimum of fuss. No shock, no rear suspension, just fat, knobby tires, a wide range of gears, and really awesome brakes.

Hardtails still exist—they've just taken a back seat to suspension. If you want to increase your handling skills, try riding without suspension, and negotiating all the ruts, logs, bumps and holes in the trails or fire roads. Just don't attempt to catch your buddies as they fly away on their "suspendo" (full-suspension) bikes, because you won't be able to beat them on the downhill.

These sturdily built bikes with knobby tires will go anywhere you can pedal them. They are like jeeps on two wheels, ready to cruise over debris, jump logs, and negotiate singletrack. Since this bike is considered low-end, as opposed to more expensive high-end models, you may discover that after three or four hours of riding your body feels like a wet noodle. The gears shift, they just don't shift quickly or smoothly. You can climb the mountain, but it feels as though you're lugging twenty pounds of luggage.

Regular mountain bikes look like their stylish counterparts that are manufactured with full chrome-moly or aluminum frames. Since they do not have the high-end component gruppos, or frames made with the lightest

Fig. 7-2. Julie in upright riding position, pulling a trailer.

materials, these bikes won't perform as well as a serious off-road rider would prefer.

However, for short excursions into the woods, fast and aggressive city riding, and basic around town cruising, these bikes are a great buy. You'll become proficient at riding, due to your stretched-out position on the bike. You'll discover new muscles from attempting rides normally beyond your ability. You'll be able to follow your children around on their BMX bikes, negotiating every treacherous ditch as well as they do. And then you'll probably want to upgrade to a high-end mountain bike.

Compared with the low-end version, the high-end mountain bike has a lighter frame, better quality components, and the ability to take its rider far into the wilderness without doing a lot of huffing and puffing. This is because these bikes are designed to optimize your pedal stroke, meaning that every revolution of the pedals puts your energy to good use. Low-end mountain bikes often absorb part of the rider's pedaling energy because the frames are not built of optimal material, or the bottom bracket flexes. High-end mountain bikes transmit as much pedal power as possible directly to the drivetrain, allowing you to work less and get more for your efforts.

These bikes will travel over any terrain. They are the premium choice for the serious trail rider. Mountain bikes are built to withstand the rigors of serious off-road riding. Some are designed with a steeper seat tube angle, which places the rider over the handlebars. Others, particularly old style, are designed with a relaxed seat tube angle, which keeps you comfortable for long periods of time, and makes descending just a little less hairy. Whichever high-end mountain bike you ride, you should be stretched-out more in the 90-degree angle for optimal climbing and descending. Plan to stay in the woods for hours once you get used to riding this type of bike. You'll love it forever.

Mountain Bikes with Front Suspension

Front suspension on your trusty hardtail allows you to take trail riding one step further and ride deep into the forest, desert, or pasture. Rather than slow down and roll over wet tree roots or water bars, you can simply ride right into them. The shock will dampen each and every bump, saving your wrists and hands from taking any abuse. I recommend that you first become proficient at bike handling skills before buying a bike with suspension. If you do not learn how to ride a suspension-less mountain bike off-road, you may find yourself attempting trails beyond your capability. This could lead to disaster if you do not choose your ride, and your riding partners, carefully.

Suspension will allow you to keep up with the gnarly dudes who regularly mangle their bikes and their bodies on limitless obstacles and intense singletrack. Unless you are willing to be similarly mangled, pick your line carefully, and descend with all due caution. Picking a line means looking at least 20 feet ahead of your bike while descending, then riding that line. This is a skill that will save you countless hours of stopping and starting. Once you've looked, you can plan ahead, and avoid the worst spots on the trail, such as huge ruts, deep holes, and hidden logs.

Full-Suspension Bikes

Full suspension is an extension of front suspension, and works especially well in downhill riding. If you are an experienced rider and plan to speed down the mountain on a regular basis, full suspension is the only way to go. Rather than negotiate anything, you can simply cruise at warp speed and hope you never go down. The full-suspension bikes can handle almost anything, except of course, the aforementioned huge ruts, deep holes, and hidden logs.

Unless you have many hours logged in technical singletrack riding, I don't recommend buying a full-suspension bike. If you are going to ride really easy trails, that's another matter, but if you plan to buy the bike, then plummet down the nearest ski slope, you will possibly become injured. The full-suspension bike makes you feel like bumps in the road don't exist when they really do. Even though these bikes are fun to ride, they may lull you into believing you can ride over anything. Learn how to negotiate technical singletrack before you get into downhill riding.

Suspension bikes are primarily built for speedy down-hilling on trails and fire roads. They are a good choice if you like to go fast on long descents, and if they have a dial with which you can stiffen the suspension for the uphills. Knobby tires, full-on gearing, triple chainrings, and lots of cushion keep you comfy in even the most treacherous terrain. Your back won't hurt, your butt won't hurt, your wrists won't hurt, your neck won't hurt. The full suspendo is a premium way to kiss the sky, ride the mountain, and easily descend through the muddy waterbars of the East, or the dry, tree-rooted singletracks of the West. Wherever the place that calls you is located, taking your suspendo mountain bike will be a sure way to enjoy the scenery and keep up with the guys. And

Fig. 7-3
Woman cyclist
in Oxford,
England.

ladies, you can really hammer with these machines, so be careful at all times, and don't attempt anything you can't finish.

Road Bikes

Road bikes are the next step to going nice and fast. They are designed to place you in your optimal position for aerodynamic efficiency. This means you'll be stretched-out over your bike in, hopefully, a 90-degree angle. You can't really ride on gravel, dirt, or large potholes. You can't really jump curbs, or negotiate gnarly singletrack. What you can do is achieve optimal climbing, descending, and straight-on power with these sleek machines. At first, your neck may hurt a little. In time, you'll get over that and begin to feel the essence of true road riding. What a thrill! Road bikes sometimes have triple chainrings on the front, with small cogs on the rear. This means that you can reach high speeds

Fig. 7-4 Women's mountain biking advocate Jacquie Phelan, riding her custom-built Charles Cunningham aluminum mountain bike with drop handlebars.

while descending, while still having low gears for climbing.

Some high-end road bikes have a relaxed frame geometry. Others have a very steep geometry. Whichever suits your riding style will be the bike for you. Do you want to scream around corners, hanging over your handlebars? Get a bike with a steep seat tube angle. Are you more interested in smooth pedaling, long distances, and more cornering room? Get a bike with relaxed frame geometry, which will put you more in the middle of the frame. Are you a time-trialing triathlete? Get a tri-bike, and trade handling for speed. Wherever you ride your road bike, stay on smooth surfaces, avoid all potholes, and carry spare tubes. Those skinny tires are the only thing between you, the road, and grit in your mouth.

Road bikes are the lean, mean, speedy machines that still dominate the roads today. Roadies are the dedicated riders who choose this bike as their favorite, wear the appropriate team jerseys, and shave their legs (especially the guys). If you are one who loves riding this squirrely beast with dropped

Fig. 7-5 Gary Fisher, one of several founding fathers of mountain biking. Photo courtesy Gary Fisher Bicycles.

handlebars and skinny tires, you should find a pack of road riders to draft with, and beat the wind.

Watch the road carefully for small debris and bumps. Unlike the mountain bike, road bikes do not tolerate obstacles. This means no trails, no dirt roads, with only the highway stretching out for miles before you. There are those who take their road bikes off-road, but in reality, road bikes cannot be safely ridden anywhere except on smooth paved roads. The riders are in an aerodynamic position, which facilitates speed, but creates neck aches in the inexperienced. Learning to ride in a pack will increase your stamina, mileage and speed, as well as teach you the finer points of non-verbal communication on the bikes.

8

How to Get Your Bike Serviced at the Shop

Whatever you do, clean that puppy off before you take it anywhere for servicing. Everyone's bike gets dirty, and with a little bit of effort, you'll have a sparkling clean bike in no time. Regular maintenance includes periodic gunk removal. You can wear dishwashing or heavy duty rubber gloves if you want to protect your nails and skin.

Cleaning Your Bike

If your faithful steed is filthy, hose it off with a garden nozzle, and get the large chunks of mud off the brakes and drivetrain. Next, wipe the bike down with a clean rag, and spray the drivetrain with WD-40, or some other water-displacing potion. After the drivetrain has had a chance to sit and rest, wipe everything that moves, such as chain, cogs, and crankset. Use a dirty rag for this odious chore. Clean the derailleur pulleys with a toothbrush to get all the grit out. Wipe down the entire bike until everything sparkles. Do you still have a problem that needs to go to the shop, or was it the mud between your derailleur pulleys?

Getting Work Done at the Shop

When you have ascertained exactly what your bike needs done—such as bottom bracket adjustment, wheel truing, headset adjustment, derailleur or brake adjustment, part replacements, what have you—make a list for when you speak with the mechanics. You'll need it.

Hand the shop a totally clean bike, take out your list, and ask the mechanic to give you an estimate before you drop off your bike. Ask them what day you'll have your bike back, too. Some shops get behind on repairs during the busy season, and may not have your bike back in time for the next ride you have planned. If you need to order part replacements, you should probably continue to ride the bike, unless the parts in question are so damaged that you can't ride the thing anymore. You may wind up waiting weeks for the new parts to come in, while your poor bike languishes in repairland, waiting for its fix.

Fig. 8-1 Kate trues a wheel at The Spoke in Williamstown, MA.

A typical repair item that you shouldn't attempt for the first time at home, especially without the proper tools, is a wheel true. Let's say your new bike's wheels go out of true within a month after you bought it. Chances are, you'll hear a "ping, ping" as you pedal. This occurs because the wheel wasn't stress-relieved at the shop, and now that you have applied radial torque (by pedaling), the wheel is stress-relieving itself. The only problem is, that wheel will go out of true if each and every spoke isn't just absolutely perfect the first time it was built, which is not likely. So off you go to the shop with your bike and your sales receipt.

Shop Talk

Find someone who looks as though he is in charge, and show him your complete bike. Spin the wheel, then say this:

"Hi. My name is (your name), and I bought my bike a month ago. Look at this wheel." Spin, spin. "What do you think?"

The guy will probably say, "Oh yeah, that looks like it's definitely out. When did you buy it?" At that point, you pull out your receipt, and show him. "This is a warranty tune-up deal, so we won't charge you anything," he'll say. "I'd better get a mechanic to look at this." And off he'll run to pass the buck to the nearest mechanic. So much for that guy. Here comes the mechanic. Spin the wheel again.

He'll probably say, "Wheel's out, huh? Who built this bike, anyway?" You can probably find the initials of the mechanic who built your bike on the receipt, but that doesn't matter one bit. What matters is that you want your wheel trued on the spot, and they are backed up for a week with repairs.

Try the soft approach: "Well, as you can see, this wheel is out. And it really doesn't matter to me that it wasn't stress-relieved while the bike was being built, because now you are here and you can treat this wheel the way it should have been treated in the first place." He'll blink at the word "stress-relieved" because that's your password into his world.

He may say, "Uh, yeah, huh, but we're like, really booked up for the next week." Which he is, but so what? Kick into high gear:

"Yo, dude, I get it that you are busy, but my wheel really needs a good stress-relieving, not just truing, and I hate to complain, but you know, if you can just take care of this now, we won't mention it again." Then, offer him a cappuccino or something, just to take the edge off. "Why don't I step out and grab you a cookie, hot chocolate, coffee, tea, while you spend a little time getting to know my wheel? And then when I ride it again, it won't go ping, ping anymore." Hand him the wheel, and take off. Bring him back a goodie, and chances are, your wheel will have new life.

No mechanic wants to admit sloppy workmanship, but sometimes it happens. Here's another example of how to get what you want at the shop. This time, you think you need a new drivetrain because your old one is old, the chain slips, and the chainrings and cogs are missing teeth. Back to the same shop you go, bike in hand.

"Hey there," you say to the nearest friendly looking mechanic. "I've got a problem and I'd like some advice." He'll look over, interested because you chose him and didn't whine. "Want to take a looksie?" Hand over the bike. "Put it on the stand and I'll show you the problemo," you say. "Shift the gears and watch the chain jump." He'll shift away, and probably notice your drivetrain is trashed.

"Yup. You need to shell out some cashola and replace your chainrings, rear cogs, and chain." He takes the bike down and heads back to work. At least your suspicions are verified.

"Well, can I have an estimate for the parts and service to install them?" you ask. He may shake his head, because that may not be his territory, and you may have to find a salesperson, or the manager to actually place an order. If he answers, it will probably go something like this:

"New drivetrain in XT will cost you ..., LX will cost you ..., Dura-Ace will cost you ..., depending on what you need." Get an estimate of installation costs, too. If they do not have the parts in stock, choose which parts you want to buy (try to upgrade your old parts with better ones), fill out an order form, pay a deposit, and prepare to wait for a couple of weeks. Take your bike with you and ride it until you get your replacement parts. Ride it unless the old parts have ceased to function and cannot be adjusted any further. If teeth are missing, park your bike.

Anything you need done—whether it is a new stem replacement, a derailleur adjustments, toeing-in brakes (toe-in means proper brake pad placement to prevent squealing), wheel truing, drivetrain replacements, or a shock rebuild—will go smoother if you first ascertain what is wrong with your bike, then expect to pay the shop for their time. I recommend doing all of your work at home, but not everyone is mechanically inclined, nor do they want to be, so the bicycle shop is the place you need to patronize for any repairs. Educate yourself with a good bike repair manual, even if you never touch a wrench. You'll find your reading and riding experience enables you to quickly diagnose your problem, then take the patient to the doctor for its medication.

Try to stick with the shop where you originally bought your bike. They'll appreciate your continued patronage, become willing to discuss minutia with you, and know how to service the particular model you own. If there are ever any warranty issues concerning your frame, the shop will be able to interface with the bike's manufacturer and replace it if it must be replaced. I also recommend treating the underpaid mechanics to an occasional latte. They'll take special care of your bike if you are nice to them. They may even speed it out if you have a ride to attend and are a regular customer.

Remember, bicycling is a sport that requires a certain amount of finesse. You first find the shop, figure out the ride, fit yourself, buy the bike, ride the bike, and repair the bike. It's like having a new friend around who will take you to far-away lands and distant horizons. There you will meet exciting people and have wondrous adventures. Take care of your bike, and it will take care of you.

And ride safely so we can all be around for tomorrow.

Bibliography

Cuthbertson, Tom. *Anybody's Bike Book: An Original Manual of Bicycle Repairs*. Berkeley, CA: Ten Speed Press, 1984.

Hershon, Maynard. *Tales from the Bike Shop*. Brattleboro, VT: Vitesse Press, 1989.

Savage, Barbara. *Miles from Nowhere: A Round-the-World Bicycle Adventure*. Seattle, WA: The Moutaineers, 1987.

Stuart, Robin and Cathy Jensen. *Mountain Biking for Women*. Waverly, NY: Acorn Publishing, 1994.

Terry, Georgiana. *Terry Bicycle Owner's Manual*. Macedon, NY: Precision Cycling for Women, 1998.

Van der Plas, Rob. *Mountain Bike Maintenance: Repairing and Maintaining the Off-Road Bicycle*. San Francisco, CA: Bicycle Books/Motor Books International, 1998.

Van der Plas, Rob. *Road Bike Maintenance: Repairing and Maintaining the Modern Lightweight Bicycle*. San Francisco, CA: Bicycle Books, 1997.

Willard, Frances. *How I Learned to Ride the Bicycle*. Sunnyvale, CA: Fair Oaks Publishing Company, 1991.

Index